Steven Bruce

WILT

1987 Books

This paperback edition published 2024
by 1987 Books

1987books.info@gmail.com

First Edition

A CIP record of this book
is available from the British Library

ISBN: 978-1-8380885-2-1

Cover illustration: Wilt, *acrylic on paper,*
by Malgorzata Bruce, 2024

OTHER WORKS BY STEVEN BRUCE

Poetry:

White Knuckle

Caffeine

AWARDS & NOMINATIONS

Winner of the Chiron Book Award

Winner of the Firebird Book Award

For the reader,
who breathes life into these pages.

CONTENTS

Contents

It is not events that disturb people,
it is their judgements concerning them.

— EPICTETUS

WILT

Survival Is Smiling at the Elements

By now, I should be pushing heroin
into my groin, pickling my kidneys in vodka,
ditching dismembered bodies in remote lakes,
or hopping aboard the suicide express.

When your first childhood memory
is of masked men bursting into the squat,
fighting with your drug-dealing father,
and almost falling on top of you.

When you see your father accusing
your mother of poisoning his food
and splitting her scalp
with a dinner plate.

When he beats her most nights,
berates her most nights, strips
away what little dignity
her parents left her,

and you're too small and useless
to protect her from anything.

When you witness a schoolmate hit
by a train one blue-skied afternoon,
and you get an unwanted insight
into what colours our interiors.

When your father dies alone
and rots for a week before
anybody cares to find
his yellow body.

When your mother falls into bed
with broken men, and one worms
his way in by seducing her
with pills and powder.

When he beats you most days,
berates you most days, strips
away what little dignity
your parents left you,

and you're too small and useless
to protect yourself from anything.

When you're ten years old
and covered in lumps, bruises,
untreated wounds, dried blood,
and no one kisses you goodnight.

When you discover your mother's
checked herself out of the inferno,
and there's nowhere for you to go
but through deeper circles of hell.

When you're left alone to carry
the weight of failed parents,

When you're fourteen years old
and thrown out onto the streets
like the bloody offal
of a mediaeval butcher,

and before you know it,
you're surviving with junkies,
winos, thieves, prostitutes,
and future murderers.

When you're slashed open
with an eight-inch kitchen knife
and your wound's red lips laugh
at you with a silent insanity.

When you're stuck in a foster home,
and the carer plays you a videotape
of German girls groaning as giant
genitalia glide in and out of them,

and you think, *There's no place*
sacred from the beast of man.

When you read in the paper
that the college girl you dated
got killed by a knife-wielding,
amphetamine-addled maniac.

When your friend kills himself
because he couldn't cope
with the fact it was his alcoholic
mother who stole his virginity.

When you understand starlight
is dying out, and the cosmic
void will stand victorious.

As absurdity careens
like fields upon fields
of golden sunflowers.

As our black dogs howl in unison.

As the soul strides on
despite its fractured ankles.

By now, I should be pushing heroin
into my groin, pickling my kidneys in vodka,
ditching dismembered bodies in remote lakes,
or hopping aboard the suicide express.

But by some miracle,
I am still here, lucid,
without addiction,
opposing the odds

for those of us
who passed through the steel
jaws of this apathetic
meat grinder.

And I
am light-years away from invincible.

And I
have developed no superpowers.

And I
wear no golden mythical armour.

And I
have exhumed no forgotten secrets.

And I
hold no sacred treaty with the gods.

Each day, I rise and tread out
into the world's feral wilderness
with a smile
and calm fortitude,
despite its extreme elements.

Wilt

So when the cruel
winter thawed,
I looked up close to see
my heart
as a frost-bitten berry.

And my caring leaves
had wilted on the vine.

And those sentinel prickles
rose as spear tips to protect
the last of my bearing fruit

from the cleaving
of cutlass cunts.

Poetics

How to say it?

When forms become overworked
and demand a vacation.

When internal and end rhymes
are sick to death of each other
and file for divorce.

When similes are fumbled
with more times than a cheap
escort's labia.

When iamb, trochee,
dactyl, and anapaest
march off to die
in the blood-soaked trenches
of a distant war.

When sentimentality leaps
from the top of a skyscraper.

When inverted sentences
swing from the gallows.

When mixed metaphors
digest in the iron stomach
of a turkey vulture.

When a rose
is a rose is a rose.

How to say it?

When the heart
no longer cares
to refine itself.

When the soul's
almost out of steam,

and there's enough
foresight inside of you
to admit that in a hundred years
none of your matters
will matter.

How to say it?

When inspiration's
as ripe and fragrant
as wilted flowers.

When the flash of a rat's tail
vanishing beneath your bed
holds more fear
than a lightning bolt

splitting apart
a distant oak tree.

When everything's
already spoken.

How to say it?

When you are not Blake.
When you are not Shakespeare.
When you are not Keats.

When you are contradicting components
stumbling through this dog-eat-dog cosmos.

How to say it?

When you believe
poetry, like air,
is for all
human beings.

How to say it?

In your own simple way,
I guess.

Where Are the Sonnets?

She said, *None of your poems rhyme,*
and where are the sonnets?

Oh, but life's rhythms
aren't written in syllable counts.

Nor is our iron forged
by trite rhyme schemes.

At worst, man's form
is a hurricane colliding
with an erupting volcano.

At best, it's a night of music,
libation, and a partner he adores
climaxing at the end of his tongue.

Man is a simple beast grazing
in fields of dissonance.

He never stops
to appreciate the flowers

because they never stop
to appreciate him.

And his mind's a gun chamber
loaded with infernal reflections.

Entity and Nonentity

Darkness.

This poem will end
with darkness.

As before its birth,
before it lived, laughed,
loved, and knew loss.

This poem will end,
as it started,

with darkness.

First Star I See Tonight

It emerges
like a pimple on the night sky's chin.

Make a wish.

What's there to lose
but time and sanity?

Confess.

What longings billow
your heart's sails
tonight?

To win a jackpot
            other than birth?

Something ample,
right?

Enough to forget
about the cost
of living?

To have a figure fashionable
for the modern age?

To be famous?
To be successful?
To be happy?

To be enough
for them not to walk
out on you?

World peace?
        Don't lie.

For your enemies
to wake as dung beetles?

        Yes.

For a teaspoon
of self-confidence?

For a room
with a clear view
of the singing ocean?

To be young?
To be old?
To be somebody
or anybody else?

To feel loved?

You don't need much,
do you?

Only

to wake up
to one person pleased
to see you.

Some nights,
if you listen with intent,
you can hear humanity's desires
resound around Venus
and disappear
into the unapproving universe.

Everyday, a Fragment

As our lives sweep
from ample time
to memorial,
the beautiful everyday
passes
like a swift wind.

And our looming tombs
will forever blind us
from the rising moon
and everything else
our hearts
have taken for granted.

Kippers

How defeated we are.

Caught and strung
out like so many kippers
drying out in a snarling sun.

Someone somewhere
persuaded us that victory
lies in popularity
and material wealth.

And without it,
we are social pariahs.

So we work beyond burnout,
play less, wake early, and feel
inadequate anyway,

despite designer
nails, handbags,
suits, and watches.

How defeated we are.

To be the respiring dead,
wilting in shallow graves
lying at the denouement
of our own shovels.

How defeated we are.

To cling to hopelessness
like it's the handrail
on hell's rickety
roller coaster.

How defeated we are.

Yet there remains
a wild resilience
in us.

I've seen it
in an unemployed,
seven-stone woman
raising three children
alone.

I've seen it
in a muscle-bound behemoth
holding back tears of childhood
abuse until he thinks no one
is around to hear him cry.

I've seen it
in a fifty-six-year-old warehouse
workhorse with arthritic joints
and two minor strokes
under his belt.

I've seen it
in a jolly pensioner
living out her final days
with metastatic lung cancer
in a gloomy care home.

How defeated we are.

Yet there remains
a wild resilience
in us,

something cash and celebrity
can't afford.

And its voice
thunders
from the gut.

Telling us,

Go on.
Go on.
Go on,

for one more day.

Midnight Verse XVI

As we deem ourselves
architects of fate,

the cool moon laughs,

and the universe
unfolds as it does,

in perfect chaos.

How to Pass Time While Waiting for the Nuclear Apocalypse to Melt What's Left of Your Brain

Perfect the fine art
of poached eggs on toast.

Gauge how high you can piss
in the wind while whistling
Beethoven's Für Elise.

Win all the imaginary arguments
raging inside your head.

Rehearse your everything's okay smile
in a mirror of dirty dishwater.

Walk into a glass door
and apologise to it for your lack
of spatial awareness.

Practice cunnilingus
on an origami vagina.

Suck absinthe
from your lover's
belly button.

Attend gatherings
with people you have nothing
in common with.

Dye your pubic hair
neon pink.

Try to outrun
your shadow
before it garrottes you.

Count your teeth
while defecating.

Don't waste time washing your hands.
Scientists say there's faecal matter
everywhere.

Devise the perfect retort
to an insult you received
three years ago.

Put your trust in experts,
for they are never wrong.

Believe in the news,
for it is the new religion.

Put your faith
in the government,

for they hold your welfare
at the forefront of their coal hearts.

Shave your toes
with a straight razor.

Squat bare-arsed over a mirror
to see if your anus
needs bleaching.

Call up your ex incognito
to congratulate them on winning
first place in the annual
bulldog licking piss from a nettle
lookalike competition.

Regret nothing.

Take part in a social
media challenge.

The one where you set
yourself on fire
and bleat like a sheep.

How harmful can it be
if others are doing it?

Learn to juggle
mouldy tangerines.

Buy a pet rock.

Dress it in a blonde,
shaggy wig,
and name it dumbfuck.

Swipe a tenner
from your granny's purse
and invest it
in something lucrative
like shoe umbrellas, cat wigs,
diet water, glass hammers,
or the goddamned
twirling spaghetti fork.

And don't get befuddled
by a middle-class morality.

The old bint would only waste
it at the bingo or on cheap sherry
or slip it into a birthday card
and forget to mail it to you.

Chant the bandwagon mantra,

It's vital to fit into
the sweaty armpit
of society.

Trot out on an old nag
towards the windmills
of absurdity.

Stock up on sunscreen
and tinned goods.

Build up a tolerance
to radiated root vegetables.

Ask the gospel internet
which style of self-defence is best
to kill a rabid two-headed bear.

Sell enough organs
to buy a house
outright.

One with a metal bathtub.

So when the shaboom comes,
your carcass can spend an eternity
doing a canned sardine impression.

Make a quick call.

Inquire about nuclear blast
homeowner's insurance.

Some devious three-eyed cunt's
bound to be selling it.

Peace on Earth Will Come

When goldfish tread mountains.
When lions gorge on broccoli heads.
When death picks a life insurance policy.

When God strips homo sapiens
of their inherent hatred.

When Mother Earth
learns that only radiated roaches
and rubble survived.

With Notes of Irony

Call it being dogged by bad luck.
    Call it a fool's prophecy.
Call it fate lighting a cigarette
    after it fucks you in the arse.
Call it an albatross around your neck.
    Call it an ancestral curse.

Blame it on crossing paths with a black cat.
    Blame it on your astrological sign.
Blame it on the neighbour who dabbles
    in witchcraft. Blame it on the devil.
Blame it on your treacherous spouse
    for opening an umbrella
inside the house. Blame it on a bad penny.
    Blame it on a broken mirror.
Blame it on the politician you elected.
    Blame it on old age.
Blame it on the youth of today.

Say to yourself that you deserve it all.
    Say it with gusto.
Say it's one giant goat rodeo.
    Say it's too late to turn it around.
Say it while donning the paint of a tragic clown.
    Say it with self-entitlement.

But for pity's sake, never say
    it's the sum of your choices.

Ars Absurdia

Each absurd opinion
enlists a warband
to protect it.

And no matter how ignorant
or foolish it may be,

the warriors ride out
blindfolded on dead horses,
impervious to arrows of reason.

If

If only wasted time was a boomerang.

If only God had blessed
you with some talent.

If only you had a million years
to discover your calling.

If only your family and friends
would believe in you.

If only you had a Viking's courage.

If only the odds of success
were a hundred per cent.

If only you had enough money
and knew the right people.

If only you could lift the curse
of caring about what others think.

If only you knew where to begin.

If only you had teachers
who could inspire you.

If only the stars
would realign themselves.

If only your time wasn't
plagued with folderol.

If only Lady Luck was on your side.

If only you had the sense to say,
    Forget all of that.
    This is a finite tree of life,
    and the branches are mine
    to shake any way
    I goddamn
    please.

Your Best Days Are Waiting

But first, your parents need time
to fuck you up, to hand down irrational
behaviours, and to blame your arrival
for their unfulfilled lives.

But first, learn how to spell
antidisestablishmentarianism,
to blow and finger the recorder,
the unbearable steps of long division,
and other fundamental life skills.

But first, in the folly of youth,
define your future.

But first, a new house on finance,
a luxury car on finance, the latest phone
from a Chinese sweatshop on finance,
a ready-made life on finance to chain
you to that soul-strangling nine-to-five.

But first, blame time
for moving on without you.

But first, let addiction take precedence.
Hard liquor, deep-fried chicken and ice
cream from a bucket, opioids, oniomania,
cocaine sniffed from a waxed snatch,
or risk it all in a shaky hand of pontoon.

But first, leather jackets, symbolic tattoos,
and blue pills to bolster your libido.

But first, dreams deferred, bitterness
at the lives of others, hatred towards
friends and family, and complaints that no
one wants to spend time with you.

But first, old age, osteoarthritis,
chronic obstructive pulmonary disease,
diabetes, hearing loss, cataracts,
and deathbed
regrets.

Bout

There are no
lasting victories.

Only fears of the future,
absurdity, bouts of joy and rain,
a wilting red rose,
lucky blows,

and

an unexpected
call from death.

Self-Portrait with Belongings

Too often, I sit alone at this small desk
in the corner of my room.

Nestled amongst my white
coffee-encrusted cup, cigar butts,
settled ash debris, matchsticks
stacked like half-burnt
witch cadavers, books
on writing, paper
scraps containing stoic
quotes, and questions written
in crude handwriting,

If God created man in his own image,
why are we such savages?

The text cursor blinks at me
with such apathy
as my knuckle scars
flash in the lamplight
like little lightning bolts.

My careful fingers push out words
from places I seldom know.

There are nights
when I write
a line that makes me feel
like Goya's lone colossus.

Then I turn my gaze
to the stars
burning out in the cosmic void,
and I'm right back
to being a significant nobody.

Too often, I sit alone at this small desk
in the corner of my room.

As the clock's hands flood forward,
I write towards dusty death.

While families family.
While parties party.
While orgies orgy.

While gigs gig
on without me.

And my solitary heart
would have it no other way.

Finding Rhythm

Shut
heaven's
golden eye.

The night agrees with me most.

When the ocean of faces calms
and I can retreat to the restful silence
of an empty seashell.

To be alone. Reading by lamplight.

As Falstaff laps
at the cream of life.
As Don Quixote barrels
towards outlandish windmills.
As Dante slips by a thousand faces
made purple by cold.

How the old tales know us better
than we care to know ourselves.

To sip strong coffee
between pages.

To be an apparition
of a face in the crowd.

To flee the tech deluge
that strips us of humanity.

If only for a sacred evening.

Let me remember
to always get lost
in the rhythms of life
and not in the dissonance
of existence.

And So

And so the hours fade.
And so life at times
appears futile and absurd.

And so the flesh withers.
And so you ask your waning soul,
        Am I doing what's right?

Ghost

To roam a silent sea, sweeping
as far as the eye can see.

To be crude salt in the cold,
blue lungs of Icarus.

To be a forgotten rabbit
in the magician's black hat.

To be an invitation lost in the post.

To be a mite muscling through
the dust of day-to-day life.

To be a plump callus
on the clammy palm of Sisyphus.

To be a feast spoiling in the hall
of some forgotten king.

Midnight Verse XIX

Let's run away.

Leave society
with its hang-ups.

It's only fit
for the gallows
anyway.

Let's carry the remains
of our hearts outside
and revel in the lone
moon's splendour.

This River of Ours

FOR MALGORZATA BRUCE

At midnight,
we wander by
the Arno River.
Moon bright. Ink clouds
are swift.
A dark water
symphony
streams
into our ear canals.
The night's transient.
Love respires.
Arm in arm,
you are as near
to me as a lover
could be.
Despite acrid blue
smoke rising
from my cigar's
tip.
despite grief
scorching
my soul's edges.
Moonlight creeps
in
and out
of the clouds
in silent Firenze.
And I find
myself
lost

      in this river
      of ours.
Because
      days exist when
            I believe
I am unlovable
      and was born
to be hammered
            down
      into the rotten
timber
      of the world.
      And here you are,
            proving me
                  wrong.

Transient

It's nights
like this when the Earth's
dark and serene,

I sink into its inky
swell of anonymity.

Along with the woodworm beetles
boring holes in my antique
rocking chair.

Along with the cluster
of tiny spiders
poised, hunting flies
by the bathroom light.

As the majestic mundane
becomes disregarded,

time's
swift tide
rolls over us
in a subtle way.

Night after night,

another poem,
another sawdust head,
another snared fly.

Night after night,

another air pocket's picked
from our precious lives.

It's nights
like this when the Earth's
dark and serene,

I catch a breath
while my head still
smiles above water.

Like a Dog Chasing Cars

She was in her mid-twenties,
had two kids with different dads,
and smelled like an unplugged
fridge.

Her first sperm donor killed
an infant while drunk driving.

Her second got caught fingering
a sleeping pre-teen and fled before
anyone could boot his teeth
through his lips.

On summer evenings,
we flocked like sheep
without a Border Collie.

We drank cheap booze
around a small garden bonfire
made of household trash.

And as the flames quivered,
she would say, *All men are shit. All of 'em.*
Don't need 'em. Never did. 'Specially since
I got me eight-inch dildo at home.

And we would all laugh.
And drink more cheap wine.
And someone would toss something
onto the fire. And we watched it burn

into nothingness like so many nights.

The following summer,
we found ourselves back
around the same fires.

But now that she had a new man,
she would say, *He's the best. I deserve it.*
He works. He cooks. He takes us places
on the weekends. He loves 'em kids
like they were his own. I always knew
a good one would come along.

And our nights passed without significance
until a coke dealer from down south
came sniffing around.

He scratched his crotch by the fire
and said, *Fuckin' caught somethin'*
from the girl who pays with her pussy.

And the hours filled with his spurious
stories before he slipped her a tiny white wrap.

And she paid him
by sucking his scabby cock,
in sight of everyone,
while her new man
and kids slept in a lightless
house across the street.

Day Shift Fragment

Said he needed work that paid more.
Said the beamer payments come first.
Said his father wanted him to move out.
Said he got a gram for his thirtieth birthday.
Said his mother packed the wrong sandwiches.
Said he needed work that paid more.
Said the doctor prescribed cream
for his genital warts.

Said the Korean escort was worth half
his wage to make him feel wanted
for one hour a week.

The Unmeaning of Life

Without meaning,

we are swine
careening
inside

the abattoir's
shadow.

Bottled Laughter

It's been almost seven years
since that forgotten day
in the hobby shop.

I was buying paint brushes
to blush a miniature
dragon's scales

when I overheard the cashier's
rant about the height
of his new chair.

I approached the counter.

He sat there with spectacles and a rosy smile,
weighing in at over twenty stone.

When I gave him the brushes,
he said something humorous.

For the life of me,
I can't recall what it was.

As he chuckled at his own joke,
he leaned back, and the stool gave
out from underneath him.

By some divine miracle,
I kept a straight face
while saying the only thing
you could say in this situation,

Are you alright, mate?

He clambered to his feet,
cursed, and scowled at the stool
with his hands on his rotund hips.

I bought the brushes, fled the shop,
and continued to contain my laughter.

On my way home,
I recalled the time I tripped
in the street, my chin and hands
slapping off the rough road.

How I shot up
like a lightning bolt in reverse,
fearing someone had seen.

And it's tonight,
while stargazing
and trying to find the words,
that this memory
chooses to flash
in my mind's eye.

I swear, my lips almost tear
as I laugh so hard that a tear
rolls from my eye.

And it's not at his misfortune,
the inelegant tumble, or the wild,
goat-like cry he gave.

It's the memory
of his little black boots
punting air
as he flailed on his back
like an overturned beetle.

Limits

At sundown, her father
drinks beer and blends vodka
with store-bought juice.

Within an hour, he hunches
forward and gurgles like a helpless
two-month-old baby.

And I say, *He's fucked.*

She tells me, *Leave him.*
It's what he always does.

Soon after,
he stumbles
off to bed.

I have encountered men
like this more often
than desired.

Men carried legless
from dank bars.

Men passed out in piss
-fermented alleys.

Men inebriated in kitchens,
living rooms, and gardens.

Men who vomit an unhappy
life into the weary eyes
of their offspring.

Men who take pride in failure.
Measure courage in empty bottles.
Romanticise their martyrdom.

Men who brag about bad hangovers,
which is the equivalent of celebrating
explosive diarrhoea after an iffy curry.

Men who try to drown
whatever demon haunts them
rather than face it head-on.

Men with decades of experience
hitting the bottle
who still don't know how to hold
their liquor

or when to say,
finally,
enough
is enough.

A Tragedy

We are born into this world
greedy, uninformed, and confused.

How many of us remain that way
beneath the shameful glare of the sun?

Here's What Happened

One blue morning
while recovering from surgery
on a torn anterior cruciate ligament.

With my leg bound in a cast
from shin to bollocks,

I see, from my window,
the local drunk muscling
through blustery winds.

In his tattooed talon,
he grips a neon
blue carrier bag bulging
with a two-litre bottle
of cheap cider.

It swings below his knees
and splits.

His blue bottle bounces
free and rolls off the kerb.

He stoops to pick
it up,
and wooah,
over he goes
in slow motion.

He struggles
with a blurry equilibrium
against assaulting winds.

When a majestic white car
halts beside him,

this couple in shining armour
rushes out to help before noticing
he's a dastardly drunkard.

They recoil in terror
as his piss
darkens the crotch
of his light blue
jeans.

They leap back
into the comfort
of their white car
and gallop away
into the distant
sunrise,

leaving our hero
stranded
on the battlefield.

But for him,
this war's
far from over.

The old boy
musters up
the strength
to scoop up
his cider.

He rises
with potency
and carries his blue
bottle like Achilles
carried Patroclus.

And our bibulous hero
marches forth victorious,
despite the extreme elements,
along an empty road.

I blow on my brew
and think,

Everyone wants to be a hero
until there's a slight chance
of getting splashed
with a drunk's piss.

Midnight Verse XXI

Why fret existential thunders?
When all we are is a fleeting dream
between two slumbers.

All That for Only Twenty Quid

I'm in the dingy living room
with a dog that's about to give
birth any day now.

Two men speak across the room.
They sport gold sovereign rings
and faded old-school tattoos.
At a distance, their arms
look like lumps of blue cheese.

From what I hear, Druggy Dougie
has been getting temmys on tick
and owes this dealer twenty quid.

So they plot to drive him out
to the middle of nowhere,
beat the *living shit* out of him,
remove his shoes, and scour
his bare feet with a wire brush.

They finish their cigarettes
and head out, leaving me alone
with the dog.

The night grows dark.
Five mongrels slide out of her,
and she scoffs their amniotic sacs.

When the man returns,
he hands me the wire brush.
It's dappled with blood and rust.
He tells me to clean it
like he showed me.

So I fill the old metal bucket
with bleach and cold water,
and I drop the brush in to soak.

And after, I do as he says,
    Fuck off to bed.

In the morning, I get up
and ask him, *Where's the pups?*
From the couch, he opens an eye
and says, *Little shits are gone.*
Gone, I say. *Someone took them?*

No, he says. *Dead in the bucket.*
Nobody wants a mongrel.

And he falls back to sleep.
And the dog glances at me.
And what her eyes say
shatters my heart.

A week later, I return from school
to see Druggy Dougie perched
on the couch. He grins at me
with dark shadows staining
his sunken eyes.

He pays his twenty quid debt
and begs for more temmys on tick.

What about the Future?
AN EVENING WITH ORSON WELLES

Orson said,
You mean humanity's future?
Oh, I take a dim view of that.
Terribly black.

I think we're invaded by people.

There's too many of us.
And we're the only animal
on the planet
capable of some kind of semi-divinity,
but we're also obviously sick
and bent on destruction.

We now have weapons
which we are not grown up
enough to handle.

We have machines to live with
that we can't deal with
and a technology that's way
beyond us.

I don't say there's no hope.

I'm not without hope,
but it would be very hard
to be optimistic at this moment.

ACKNOWLEDGEMENTS

Acknowledgements

"Poetics" and "First Star I See Tonight" first appeared in *Carcinogenic Poetry,* "Where Are the Sonnets?" in the *Rye Whiskey Review,* "Entity and Nonentity" in *Joe Blogs Poetry Jungle,* "Everyday, a Fragment", "Midnight Verse XVI", "Peace on Earth Will Come", and "Self-Portrait with Belongings" in *Masticadores USA,* "Kippers" in *Stink Eye Magazine,* "How to Pass Time While Waiting for the Nuclear Apocalypse to Melt What's Left of Your Brain" in *Voices from the Fire,* "With Notes of Irony" and "Bottled Laughter" in *Synchronized Chaos,* "If" in *Poetry Potion*, "Your Best Days Are Waiting" in *1870 Poetry,* "Bout" in *The Blood Rag,* "Finding Rhythm", "And So", and "This River of Ours" in *Medusa's Kitchen,* "Ghost" in *Disturb the Universe Magazine,* "Transient" in *Dark Winter Literary Magazine,* "Like a Dog Chasing Cars", "Day Shift Fragment", and "Here's What Happened" in *The Beatnik Cowboy,* "The Unmeaning of Life" in *The Cherita,* "Limits" in *Lothlorien Poetry Journal,* "A Tragedy" in *The World of Myth Magazine.*

"A Tragedy" winner of the *World of Myth Magazine's M.O.M. Award,* "If" recipient of *Poetry Potion's Poem of the Day*.

"What about the Future?" is a found poem taken from an Orson Welles interview on *Tomorrow with Tom Snyder* which aired on the 8th April 1975.

As always, I would like to thank Malgorzata, Liam, and Jason for their unconditional love, support, and friendship.

Finally, a big thank you goes to Matt Wall, Bob Beagrie, Barbara Leonhard, Martin Hayes, and Peter Geddis for their generous support with the making of this book.

ABOUT THE AUTHOR

About the Author

Steven Bruce is a writer and multiple-award-winning author. His poems and short stories have appeared in numerous international anthologies and magazines. In 2018, he graduated from Teesside University with a master's degree in creative writing.
An English expatriate, he now lives and writes full-time in Barcelona.

1987 Books | Author photograph, Madrid, 2019

INDEX OF FIRST LINES

Index of First Lines

1987
Books

To find out more about this author please visit
www.stevenbrucewriter.co.uk

For book details and other information email
1987books.info@gmail.com

If you enjoyed this title,
please consider leaving a review.

Printed in Great Britain
by Amazon

54124617R00057